Five-Minute Bible Devotions

for Children

Five-Minute Bible Devotions

for Children

STORIES FROM THE OLD TESTAMENT

Written by Pamela Kennedy and
Anne Kennedy Brady

Illustrated by Amy Wummer

ideals children's books.
Nashville, Tennessee

ISBN-13: 978-0-8249-5638-7

Published by Ideals Children's Books
An imprint of Ideals Publications
A Guideposts Company
Nashville, Tennessee
www.idealsbooks.com

Library of Congress Cataloging-in-Publication Data

Kennedy, Pamela, date.
  Five-minute Bible devotions for children : stories from the Old
Testament / written by Pamela Kennedy and Anne Kennedy Brady ;
illustrated by Amy Wummer.
     p. cm.
  ISBN-13: 978-0-8249-5638-7 (spiral-bound hardcover : alk. paper)
  1. Bible stories, English—O.T.—Juvenile literature. 2.
Children—Prayers and devotions—Juvenile literature. I. Brady, Anne
Kennedy. II. Wummer, Amy. III. Title.
  BS551.3.K45 2012
  242'.62—dc23
                          2011036856

Color separations by Precision Color Graphics, Franklin, Wisconsin

Printed and bound in China

Design by Katie Jennings
Cover design by Georgina Chidlow-Rucker

For Mattie Rebecca, who taught me to believe. —P.J.K.
For Kevin, who believes in me. —A.K.B.
To Rev. George Palick. —A.W.

Leo_Jun12_2

Contents

Good Beginnings

The Beauty of God's Creation (Genesis 1:1–31)

Before there was anything at all, there was God. Because God is love, he wanted to create things that were beautiful and good. God is so powerful that he can make things just by speaking their names. So God said, "Let there be light!" And there was light. Then God said, "Let there be water and land, trees, flowers, stars, animals, and people." And everything came into being, just as God said. After God finished making everything, he said, "Everything I have made is very good." The first two people were named Adam and Eve. God told them to love each other and help one another and to take care of everything God had made. Adam and Eve lived in a beautiful garden called Eden, and every day they talked with God, their very best friend.

When we look up at the night sky, we see the beautiful stars God has made. When we walk in the forest or in a garden, we see trees and flowers, bugs and birds, and many other wonderful things God has made. Every good thing we see reminds us of God's love for us. Just like Adam and Eve, we can take care of God's world. And what is even more wonderful is that we can talk with God every day and tell him how much we love him too!

Let's talk to God: Thank you, God, for creating such a wonderful world. Please help me to take care of your world and to help the people in it. Amen.

What do you say?

- Look at the picture. Can you name the things that God made?

- Who were the first two people, and what did God tell them to do?

- What are some things you can do to take care of God's world?

- Why do you think God created such a wonderful world?

What does God say?

In the beginning God created the heavens and the earth.

GENESIS 1:1

Following the Rules

Adam and Eve in the Garden (Genesis 3:1–24)

The Garden of Eden was a wonderful place where God gave Adam and Eve everything they needed. But one day a very clever serpent came to Eve and asked her, "Did God say you could not eat fruit from the trees in this garden?" Eve said, "Oh no. We can eat from all the trees except one. God said if we eat from that tree we will be punished." But the serpent replied, "I don't think so. I think God just wants to spoil all your fun. You should not listen to God. Do what you want to do." Eve thought about what the serpent said. Then she decided to break God's rules. She and Adam both ate some of the fruit that God said not to eat. As soon as they disobeyed God, they felt afraid and ashamed. They tried to hide. But God knows everything. He was sad that they had broken his rules. God still loved them very much, but because they had disobeyed him, they had to leave his beautiful garden.

On the playground, in the park, when we go on walks, there are rules to follow. At the corner, we must wait for the WALK sign. On the playground, we must take turns. In the park, we must throw away our trash. When we break rules, we may get punished, just like Adam and Eve. Following the rules sometimes seems hard, but rules keep us safe and make things fun for everyone.

Let's talk to God: Dear Lord, thank you for loving me and wanting to keep me safe. Help me to follow your rules. Amen.

What do you say?

- Who is following the rules in the picture?

- What was the rule that Adam and Eve chose not to obey?

- What are some rules that you have to obey?

- Why do you think God and our parents want us to follow rules?

What does God say?

Jesus [said], "All who love me will do what I say."
JOHN 14:23A

God's Helper

Noah and the Flood (Genesis 6:1–8:22)

Noah loved God and always tried to obey him. One day God told Noah there was going to be a flood that would cover the whole world. He gave Noah directions to build a huge boat. Noah believed what God said, so he began building the boat. It took a long, long time. When it was finished, Noah and his family went inside the boat and brought two of every kind of animal with them. Then God shut the door. Suddenly the floodwaters came! The boat floated on the water, keeping everyone inside safe and dry. Noah and his family cared for all the animals. After many months, the floodwater dried up. God said, "Now it is time to leave the boat." All the animals and people left the boat, and Noah thanked God for keeping them safe. Then God said, "You did a good job as my helper, Noah. Look, I have made a rainbow for you! Every time you see it, remember how much I love all the people and all the animals on the earth."

God made each person and animal, and he loves every one of us. Like Noah, we are God's helpers when we take good care of the animals he has created. Some of us have pets that need to be fed and taken for walks. We can make bird feeders to help wild birds. We can protect fish by not tossing trash into the water. When we help God's creatures, it makes God happy!

Let's talk to God: Thank you, God, for all the animals you have made. Help me to treat them with kindness. Amen.

What do you say?

- Can you name the animals in the picture?

- How did Noah help God?

- How can you help take care of the animals in your neighborhood?

- Why does God want us to help take care of animals?

What does God say?

The godly care for their animals.
PROVERBS 12:10A

11

Differences

The Tower of Babel (Genesis 11:1–9)

Long ago, everyone in the world spoke the same language, ate the same kinds of food, and lived in the same place. They all wanted to stay together and do the same kinds of things. They decided to build a great city where they could all live the same way. When God saw what they were doing, he was not happy. "I want my people to live all over the world," he said. "I don't want them to be exactly the same." So God caused the people to speak different languages. Then the people scattered across the earth and settled in many different places. They found different ways of doing things and different ways of saying things. It was God's good plan for groups of people to be different from one another. Our differences make us special to God and special to each other too.

In your neighborhood or school you may see people who don't look the same as you or who use words that are different from yours. If someone is from Mexico, she may say *si* for "yes." A boy from France may say *oui* for "yes." In Japan *arigato* means "thank you," but in Hawaii people say *mahalo*. People from different places may look and speak differently, but we are all God's children. He loves us and wants us to love each other too.

Let's talk to God: Dear God, thank you for making each person different and special. Help me to enjoy many different kinds of friends. Amen.

What do you say?

- What are some differences you can see among the people in the picture?

- What are some things that make you different from your friends or neighbors?

- In the Bible story, what did God do so the people would not all be the same?

- Why do you think God wants us to be different from each other?

Hello!
Jambo!

Atlas of the World

What does God say?

Even the stars differ from each other in their glory.

1 CORINTHIANS 15:41B

Keeping Promises

God's Promise to Abraham and Sarah (Genesis 12:1–5 and 21:1–7)

Abraham and his wife, Sarah, lived in a town called Ur. One day God said to Abraham, "I want you to move away from Ur. I promise to bless you. I will give you a new land and also many children." Abraham did not know where this new land would be. He and Sarah were very old, and they had never had any children. But Abraham believed God would keep his promises, so he took his family and left Ur. After many months of traveling, God brought Abraham and Sarah to a wonderful new land. They settled in this new land, but still Abraham and Sarah had no children. Would God keep all of his promises? After waiting a long time, Sarah had a baby boy! She was so happy that she named their new son Isaac, which means "laughter." Abraham and Sarah believed that God would keep his promises to them. And God did.

God always does what he says he will do. That's why we can trust God. When we keep our promises, people can trust us too. If we say we will help someone, we should do it. When we say we will share, we should do that too. Sometimes it is hard for us to keep our promises, but God will help us if we ask him. He wants us all to be promise-keepers.

~~~~~~

Let's talk to God: Thank you, God, for always keeping your promises to me. Please help me to do what I say I will do so that I can be a promise-keeper too. Amen.

14

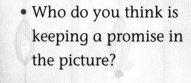

- Who do you think is keeping a promise in the picture?

- What did God promise to do for Abraham and Sarah?

- What is a promise that you have kept?

- Why do you think God wants us to keep the promises we make to others?

What does God say?

I've promised it once, and I'll promise it again: I will obey your righteous regulations.
PSALM 119:106

15

Telling the Truth

The Story of Esau and Jacob (Genesis 27:1–45)

When Isaac grew up, he married a woman named Rebekah, and they had twin sons. Their names were Esau and Jacob. One day Isaac said to Esau, "Make me a tasty stew. Then I will give you a special blessing." But Jacob wanted the special blessing for himself. He thought, *My father is very old and cannot see. If I pretend to be Esau, I can trick him. Then he will bless me instead of my brother.* So Jacob lied to his father and received Esau's blessing. When Esau came to see his father, he found out about Jacob's lie. Esau was very angry with his brother. His father, Isaac, was sad, and the whole family was upset—all because Jacob had not told the truth.

Have you ever wanted something so much that, like Jacob, you told a lie so that you could get it? Sometimes we think we can stay out of trouble by telling a lie. But after a while, people always find out. Then everyone is sad or angry, and we feel bad too. Telling the truth is sometimes hard, but it is always the right thing to do. When we tell the truth, it makes God glad.

~~~~~~

Let's talk to God:
Dear God, I am glad that you are always truthful. Please help me to be brave enough to always say what is true so that I can become more like you every day. Amen.

What do you say?

- Can you think of a time when it was hard for you to tell the truth?

- Look at the picture. Who do you think needs to tell the truth about what he did?

- Why did Jacob tell a lie to his father?

- Why do you think God is glad when we tell the truth?

What does God say?

Truthful words stand the test of time; but lies are soon exposed.
PROVERBS 12:19

Jealous or Thankful?

Joseph and His Coat of Many Colors (Genesis 37:1–4, 23–32)

Joseph lived in a big family with many older brothers. Joseph's father loved him very much and gave him a beautiful, colorful coat that Joseph wore every day. Even though Joseph's brothers had many nice things, they wanted a coat just like his. They were jealous of Joseph. The more they thought about Joseph's coat, the angrier they got. So one day they decided to get rid of Joseph and his coat! They grabbed Joseph and pushed him down into a big hole. Then they saw some travelers. They pulled Joseph out of the deep hole and sold him to the travelers so that the travelers would take Joseph far, far away. When Joseph was gone, they took his beautiful coat and ruined it.

When we want what someone else has, we sometimes feel angry just like Joseph's brothers. This is called jealousy. It is easy to be unkind when we are jealous. We forget that God loves us and that he has given us many wonderful things too. We also forget that God wants us to be kind to others and especially to our brothers and sisters. When we are thankful for what we have and treat others with kindness, God blesses us.

Let's talk to God: Dear heavenly Father, thank you for all the wonderful things you have given to me. Please forgive me when I am jealous of others. Help me to be kind to them instead. Amen.

What do you say?

- In the picture, who looks unhappy and jealous?

GREAT JOB!

- What did Joseph's brothers do because they were jealous?

- Can you name some of the wonderful things God has given to you?

- Why do you think God wants us to be kind to others?

What does God say?

Be kind to each other, tenderhearted, forgiving one another.
EPHESIANS 4:32A

Forgiving Others

Joseph Forgives His Brothers (Genesis 42:6–9 and 45:4–11)

After Joseph's brothers mistreated him, Joseph was taken far away to Egypt. The strangers in Egypt were not kind to him. But Joseph kept on trusting God. After many years, Pharaoh, the king of Egypt, heard what a good man Joseph was. He asked Joseph to take care of all the food in Egypt. Then, one day, Joseph's brothers became very hungry. "There is food in Egypt," they said. "We must go there and buy some." What would Joseph do? His brothers had been mean to him. Now he had a chance to get even. He could send his brothers to jail if he wanted! But Joseph remembered how God had taken care of him. He remembered that God is forgiving. Joseph decided to do the right thing. He told his brothers he would forgive them and help them. He gave them all the food they needed. The whole family was happy again because Joseph chose to forgive.

When people do or say things that hurt our feelings, it is easy to get mad. Sometimes we want to be mean and hurt the people who hurt us. But God wants us to forgive others and be kind to them. When we forgive someone, we are not saying what they did was okay. We are just saying we are not going to hurt them back. God says he will bless us when we forgive others.

Let's talk to God: Dear Lord, I am so thankful that you forgive me when I do or say things that are hurtful. Please help me to be kind and forgiving to others too. Amen.

What do you say?

- In the picture, who needs to be forgiven?

- What did Joseph do when his brothers were hungry?

- Can you think of someone God might want you to forgive?

- Why do you think God wants us to forgive each other?

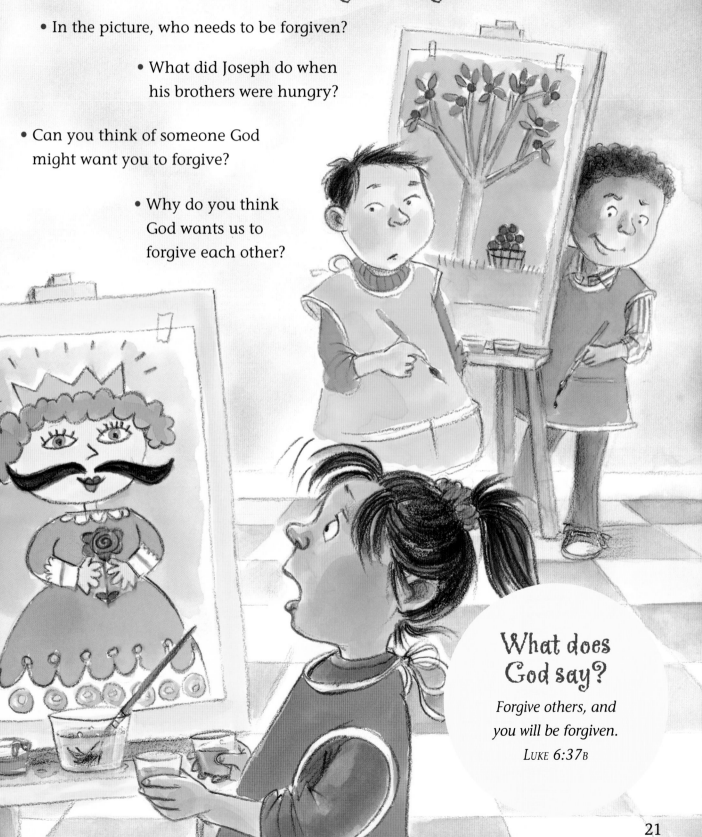

What does God say?

Forgive others, and you will be forgiven.
LUKE 6:37B

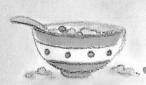

Helping Our Families

Miriam and Baby Moses (Exodus 2:1–10)

In Egypt a long, long time ago, a family had a little baby boy. They were happy, but they were also afraid. The evil king had said that all boy babies must be thrown into the Nile River! How could the family keep their baby safe? They made a special floating basket and put the baby inside. Then they hid the basket in the tall reeds by the riverbank. The big sister, Miriam, said, "I will watch the basket to make sure my baby brother is safe." Soon, a princess came to the riverbank. Walking along the water's edge, she spied the basket. "Bring that to me!" she told her helpers. They brought her the basket, and she opened it. "Oh, look! It's a sweet baby boy! I will keep him as my own son and call him Moses." Just then, Miriam came out of her hiding place. "Princess, I know a lady who will take care of the baby until he is bigger," she said. The princess smiled at Miriam and said, "That would be very good." So Miriam took little Moses home to his own mother, and she took care of him.

In families, we all need to help each other. Mothers and fathers take care of their children, and brothers and sisters take care of each other and help their parents too. God has put us in families so we aren't alone. It is one of the ways He shows his love for us. When we help each other, it makes everyone happy and pleases God too.

Let's talk to God: Thank you, God, for my family. Please help me show my love to them by being helpful and kind. Amen.

What do you say?

- Who is being a helper in the picture?

- How did Miriam help her family?

- What are some ways you help your family?

- Why do you think God wants us to be helpers in our families?

What does God say?

Always try to do good to each other and to all people.

1 THESSALONIANS 5:15B

God's Good Care

Moses Leads God's People (Exodus 16:4–18 and 17:1–7)

When Moses grew up, God asked him to do a hard job. God said, "I want you to go to Egypt and help my people there. You will lead all of them into a new land." At first Moses was afraid. He didn't know how to be a leader and take care of so many people. But God promised to be with Moses and help him. It was not an easy job. One time they ran out of food. Moses asked God for help, and God sent special food called manna to the people. Another time they were thirsty, and Moses could not find any water. He asked God for help, and God showed Moses where to find water. Every time Moses asked God for help, God kept his promise. He took good care of Moses and all the people.

God cared for Moses, and God cares for you too! When you are lonely or afraid, you can tell God, and he will comfort you. When you have to do a hard job, you can ask God to help you, and he will. When you aren't sure what to do, ask God. He will help you do what is right. Sometimes God sends help through special people like friends and family. Or he may give you a great idea so you can solve a problem. God is always there to help you because he loves and cares for you.

Let's talk to God: Thank you, God, for loving and caring for me. Please help me remember to always talk to you when I am worried or afraid. Amen.

What do you say?

- What things in the picture show God's love and care?

- How did God take care of Moses?

- Can you think of some ways you would like God to help you?

- Why do you think God takes such good care of us?

What does God say?

Give all your worries and cares to God, for he cares about you.

1 Peter 5:7

25

Taking Turns

Joshua Becomes the Leader (Joshua 1:1–9)

Moses was a very brave leader who helped God's people and told them what God wanted them to do. God gave Moses a helper named Joshua. Joshua was willing to follow Moses. He did not try to be the one who was first. He was a good follower. He listened to Moses, and he obeyed God. But one day God said to Joshua, "Now it is your turn to be the leader of my people. Don't be afraid. I will be with you wherever you go." Joshua tried to be a good leader, just like Moses. He led the people for many years, and God was always with him, just as God had promised.

When we play with friends at home or at school, it is often fun to be first. We like to be the line-leader or the first one chosen for a game. But God wants us to take turns so that everyone has a chance to be a leader and everyone has a chance to be a follower. Taking turns makes everyone feel special. Just like Moses and Joshua, whether we are leading or following, we should always do our best.

~~~~~~~~~~~~~~~~~~~~~~~~~~~

Let's talk to God: Thank you, God, for leading me in the way I should go. Help me to take turns being both a good leader and a good follower. Amen.

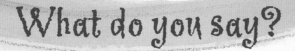

What do you say?

- Can you find a leader and a follower in the picture?

- Who followed Moses and then became a leader?

- When do you need to take turns being a leader or follower?

- Why do you think it's important for each of us to lead and to follow?

What does God say?

Jesus spoke to the people once more and said, "I am the light of the world. If you follow me, you won't have to walk in darkness." JOHN 8:12A

A Good Listener

The Story of Deborah (Judges 4:4–5)

Deborah was a woman who loved God and his people. Because Deborah was a good listener and because she wanted to help people do the right thing, God gave her a very special job. Every day, Deborah went outside the town where she lived and sat in the shade under a tall palm tree. When people had problems or disagreements, they came to talk to Deborah. They knew Deborah would listen to them and that she would help them solve their problems in a way that was fair. After Deborah heard what the people had to say, she made good suggestions about how they could get along with each other better. The people loved Deborah, and she showed she cared by listening to what they had to say.

Sometimes it is hard to listen to others. Instead, we like to tell them what we think and what we want. But good friends need to both talk and listen. When we take time to listen to others, we show them that we love them and we care about their ideas. Just like Deborah, we can help our friends and our families by taking the time to listen to them.

Let's talk to God:
Thank you, God, for giving me two ears and one mouth. Please help me to listen more than I talk, so that I can show others I care about them. Amen.

What do you say?

• Where did Deborah go to listen to the people?

• Do you know someone who would like you to listen to him or her?

• Look at the picture. Who is being a good listener?

• Why do you think God wants us to listen to one another?

What does God say?

My dear brothers and sisters: You must all be quick to listen, slow to speak, and slow to get angry.
JAMES 1:19

Cheerful Chores

Ruth and Naomi (Ruth 2:1–23)

In the town of Bethlehem, a young woman named Ruth lived with her mother-in-law, Naomi. They didn't have a lot of money to buy food, and Naomi was too old to work. One day Ruth said, "Let me go into the barley fields. I will pick up the leftover grain that falls on the ground. Then we will have something to eat." She loved Naomi and was happy to help her. So every morning, Ruth got up early and went to work in the fields. A man named Boaz owned the fields, and he noticed how cheerful Ruth was and how hard she worked. "God bless you for helping Naomi. You may work in my fields as long as you want," Boaz said. "Thank you, kind sir," said Ruth. Every day, Ruth worked hard gathering grain. And every evening, she and Naomi made that grain into a delicious meal to share.

Has your mom or dad ever asked you to clean your room or set the table for dinner? These are very important kinds of jobs called chores. In families, when everyone helps, everything runs smoothly—the house stays tidy and dinner starts on time. Just like Ruth, we can show how much we love our family by doing our chores cheerfully. It makes God happy when we do our part without complaining. So do your chores well!

Let's talk to God: Dear God, thank you for giving me special jobs to do so I can help my family. Please help me do my chores cheerfully. Amen.

What do you say?

- In the picture, find the people who are doing their chores cheerfully.

- How did Ruth help Naomi?

- What are some chores that you can do?

- Why do you think God wants us to do our chores cheerfully?

What does God say?

Work willingly at whatever you do, as though you were working for the Lord rather than for people.

COLOSSIANS 3:23

31

Answered Prayers

God Answers Hannah's Prayer (1 Samuel 1:1–20)

Hannah loved God, but she was very sad because she couldn't have a baby. She prayed every day and asked God to let her have a baby, yet no baby came. Even though she didn't see the answer to her prayers, Hannah kept right on praying. She knew that God still wanted to hear from her. Then finally, after many years, when the time was just right, God sent her a beautiful baby boy! Hannah was so happy that she sang for joy. She named her new son Samuel, which means "God hears." She wanted her family to always remember that God hears our prayers and answers us at his perfect time.

God likes it when we talk to him because he wants to hear what is important to us. He is always listening, and he always hears. And because God loves us, he answers our prayers in the way that is best. Sometimes God says "no" because what we are asking for isn't really the best thing for us. Sometimes God says "wait" because he knows that the time is not right. And sometimes God answers "yes" because he wants us to have what we are asking for. No matter how God answers, we can always know that he hears us and loves us.

Let's talk to God: Dear God, I'm glad you want us to talk to you and that you always listen. Please help me know that you will answer my prayers in a way that's best for me. Amen.

What do you say?

- Look at the picture. Can you see someone praying?

- What did Hannah pray for?

- What is something that you pray for?

- Why do you think God wants us to pray even if his answer is "no"?

What does God say?

Don't worry about anything; instead, pray about everything. Tell God what you need, and thank him for all he has done.

PHILIPPIANS 4:6

MISSING
"Tweetie"

33

Big Challenges

David and Goliath (1 Samuel 17:1–50)

One day, David saw a mean soldier who was frightening King Saul's army. His name was Goliath. He was a giant, and no one could defeat him. But David knew that God could do anything, so he told King Saul, "I will fight Goliath. The Lord will protect me." Saul decided to let him try. David took a small sling, which he had used to scare off wolves when he was a shepherd, and he walked toward Goliath. Goliath just laughed. "You can't defeat me with a sling!" he roared. David shouted back, "You may have larger weapons, but I have the power of the Lord on my side!" And with that, he put a rock in his sling and swung it around and around his head. When he let it go, the rock hit Goliath smack in the middle of his forehead. The mighty giant fell to the ground with a huge crash!

Do you ever face big challenges? Maybe it's hard to make new friends, or you're trying to learn how to do something difficult. But no problem is too big for God. God wants to help us. He loves to show us solutions we may never have thought about. So next time a challenge seems too big, try asking God to show you how to defeat it. Just like David, you will discover that with God's help, you can do very big things!

Let's talk to God: Dear God, thank you for always being near me. When I don't know what to do, please help me defeat my big problems. Amen.

What do you say?

- In the picture, who looks like she has a difficult challenge?

- Why was King Saul afraid of Goliath?

- What are some of your big problems?

- Why is it important to ask for God's help with our problems?

What does God say?

What is impossible for people is possible with God.
LUKE 18:27

Staying Calm!

Saul's Anger (1 Samuel 18:5–11)

Saul was a king who loved God, but he had a problem: he had a bad temper. Saul knew that David was very strong and wise, but after a while, Saul started to think that everyone liked David better. And that made Saul very mad. When he got mad, he lost control of his actions and made very bad choices. He shouted at David and even sent people to hurt him. One day King Saul got so angry that he threw a spear at David! David wanted to be friends with Saul, but because of the king's bad temper, it was almost impossible.

You probably know what it feels like to get angry. Maybe your heart starts to beat really fast, or you feel hot all over, or your face gets red. It's hard to stay calm at times like that! God understands that everyone gets angry sometimes, but he never wants you to lose your temper. You might throw things that can hurt people or say things that hurt their feelings. So the next time you feel yourself getting angry, try taking deep breaths and asking God to help you stay calm. When you're a little calmer, you can talk about why you got angry and think of a way to make things better. Sometimes it is hard, but God tells us to be kind to each other, even when we're angry.

Let's talk to God: Dear God, sometimes it's hard to control my temper. Please help me stay calm, even when I'm angry. Amen.

What do you say?

• Who is angry in the picture?

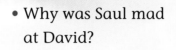 • Why was Saul mad at David?

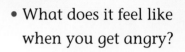 • What does it feel like when you get angry?

• Why do you think God wants us to control our anger?

What does God say?

Do not lose your temper—
it only leads to harm.
PSALM 37:8B

Good Friends

David and Jonathan (1 Samuel 18:1–4 and 19:1–7)

David's best friend was King Saul's son Jonathan. Because Jonathan was the prince, he should have been next in line to be king. But God had a different plan. He had specially chosen David to become king after Saul! This could have made Jonathan angry and jealous, but instead, Jonathan was happy for David. He loved David very much and trusted that God had great plans for his friend. David and Jonathan enjoyed spending time together. Once, when David was in danger, Jonathan helped him run away. Because of Jonathan's loyal friendship, David was safe and became one of the most powerful kings in history.

Do you have some very good friends? Good friends can cheer you up when you're sad, and they can help you celebrate when you are happy. They help each other learn new things or solve problems. Friends always want the best for each other. Sometimes your friend may receive something that you would like. Sometimes you get attention that they would like. But good friends try to be happy for each other no matter what. They treat each other with kindness. That's the way they stay friends for a long, long time.

Let's talk to God: Dear God, thank you for my good friends! Please help me to treat others like I want to be treated so that I can be a good friend too. Amen.

What do you say?

- How can you tell that the people in the picture are friends?

- How did Jonathan show he was a good friend to David?

- Can you remember a time when someone was a good friend to you?

- What are some ways you can be a good friend to others?

What does God say?

Do to others whatever you would like them to do to you.
MATTHEW 7:12A

39

Sharing

God Provides for Elijah (1 Kings 17:7–16)

Elijah was a man who loved telling people about God. One day, God asked Elijah to travel to a faraway place. When Elijah finally arrived, he met an old woman. "Will you please share some water and food with me?" Elijah asked her. "I have been walking for a long time, and I am very hungry and thirsty." Now, this woman had only a little food and water. She wasn't sure if she wanted to share with him. "What if I have nothing left for myself?" she asked. "Don't worry!" Elijah said to her. "If you share what you have with me, God will make sure there is enough for both of us." So the woman agreed. She took Elijah to her house and fixed them both a meal. Elijah stayed at the woman's house for a long time, but they never ran out of food. God made sure there was enough for everyone.

When we share what we have, it makes God happy. Sometimes that means sharing our toys and games. Sometimes it means helping those with little money or food. Sharing isn't always easy. We might feel like the old woman and think, *What if there's nothing left for me?* But God loves us very much and gives us everything we need so that we can be kind to others and share with them. And when we do, God shows us that there is enough for everyone.

~~~~~~

Let's talk to God: Dear God, thank you for giving me everything I need. Please help me share what I have with others, even when it's hard. Amen.

What do you say?

COMMUNITY CARE WEEK
HELPING OUR NEIGHBORS

DONATIONS

- Who is sharing with others in the picture?

- Why didn't the woman in the Bible story want to share?

- When have you shared something with someone?

- Why do you think God wants us to share what we have with others?

What does God say?

Don't forget to do good and to share with those in need.
HEBREWS 13:16A

41

Being Brave

Esther's Act of Bravery (Esther 4:1–17, 5:1–6 and 8:9–11)

Esther was a young woman who became a queen. One day her cousin, Mordecai, told Esther that some bad people were planning to hurt her friends and family. "Please ask the king to stop them!" he begged. But Esther was afraid. No one was allowed to talk to the king unless the king asked to see him or her first. However, Esther loved her family and friends, and most of all she loved God. So she prayed and asked God to make her brave enough to go to the king. After three days, Esther went to see the king. And when he saw how brave she was, he let her speak. The king listened to her story, and then he made a law that protected Esther's friends and family from anyone who wanted to hurt them. Esther's bravery saved many people from harm.

It isn't always easy to be brave and speak up for what is right. Maybe you want to help a friend or ask a hard question, or maybe someone is being mean and you want to ask them to stop. You might not know how to do this or what to say. But God loves you very much, and he doesn't want you to be afraid to do or say what's right. So the next time you feel scared, pray and ask God to make you brave. With God's help, you can have courage, just like Esther.

Let's talk to God: Dear Lord, thank you for loving everyone. Please make me brave enough to do and say the right thing so I can help others and be a good friend. Amen.

What do you say?

- Why did Esther need to be brave?

- Why do you think God wants us to be brave?

- Look at the picture. Who is being brave?

- Do you remember a time when you were brave even though you were afraid?

What does God say?

Be strong and courageous! Do not be afraid or discouraged. For the LORD your God is with you wherever you go.
JOSHUA 1:9B

Talking to God

Daniel and the Lions (Daniel 6:6–28)

Daniel was a man who loved God. He took time to pray three times every day. When Daniel talked to God, he told God about what he was doing. He asked God to help him make good choices, and he said "thank you" to God. But the king, who was named Darius, did not believe in God. One day he made a new law: "No one can pray to anyone but to me," he said. "If I catch anyone praying to God, I will throw him into a pit full of hungry lions!" Do you think Daniel stopped praying to God? He did not! When the king found out, he arrested Daniel and threw him in with the hungry lions. But God sent an angel to close the lions' mouths. When King Darius discovered that God had saved Daniel, he declared, "Everyone in my kingdom should pray to Daniel's God because he is the only true God!"

Just like Daniel, we can pray to God anytime we want. We can talk to God when we are happy and when we are sad. We can even talk to God when we are afraid and we don't know what to do. When we trust God and pray to him, God hears our prayers and takes care of us, just like he did for Daniel. And when we trust God, we help others believe in him too!

~~~~~~

Let's talk to God: Thank you, God, for loving me and listening to my prayers. I trust you to always hear me and answer me in the way that is best for me. Amen.

What do you say?

- Who is praying in this picture? What do you think she is saying to God?

- What happened to Daniel when he kept praying?

- When do you like to pray to God? What do you say to him?

- Why do you think God likes it when we pray to him?

What does God say?

The Lord . . . delights in the prayers of the upright.
PROVERBS 15:8B

Kindness to All

Jonah Goes to Nineveh (Jonah 1–3)

One day God spoke to a man named Jonah: "Go to the people who live in Nineveh. Tell them to stop being mean to each other. If they will ask me for forgiveness, I will help them." But Jonah didn't like the people in Nineveh. He didn't want God to help them. So Jonah sailed away on a boat instead. Suddenly there was a big storm on the sea, and Jonah ended up in the water! He began to drown, but then God sent a huge fish to swallow Jonah. Inside the fish, Jonah prayed and told God he was sorry. So God made the fish spit Jonah out onto the beach! Jonah decided to do what God wanted. He went to Nineveh and told the people how much God loved them. They believed what Jonah said, and they told God they were sorry too. Then God blessed all the people in Nineveh.

Sometimes, just like Jonah, we don't want to be kind to people who are not our friends. Maybe they have been mean to us or called us names. We might even feel like we want to be mean to them too. But God loves and cares about everyone. He wants his children to be kind to each other, even if they are not friends. This is not always easy to do, but if we ask God to help us, he will. It makes God happy when we treat everyone with kindness.

Let's talk to God: Thank you, God, for your kindness to me. Help me to show kindness to everyone I know—even to those who are not my friends. Amen.

What do you say?

- Who is being kind in the picture?

- Why didn't Jonah want to go to Nineveh?

- Can you think of someone you can treat with kindness today?

- Why do you think God wants us to be kind to *all* people?

What does God say?

A servant of the Lord must not quarrel but must be kind to everyone.
2 TIMOTHY 2:24A

ANNE AND PAMELA

K.M. Kennedy

Pamela Kennedy loves writing for children and has authored more than thirty books. In her spare time she enjoys hiking, reading, and exploring the beaches of Puget Sound. Pam and her husband currently live in Seattle, Washington.

Anne Kennedy Brady is an actress and writer in Chicago. When the stage and the laptop are dark, she enjoys rock climbing and long city walks with her husband in search of the perfect deep dish pizza.

AMY

Mark Wummer

Amy Wummer is an award-winning illustrator with over fifty children's books to her credit. Her lively watercolor illustrations for *Five-Minute Bible Story Devotions for Children* help kids relate to the Old Testament stories. She and her husband, Mark, have three grown children and live in Pennsylvania.